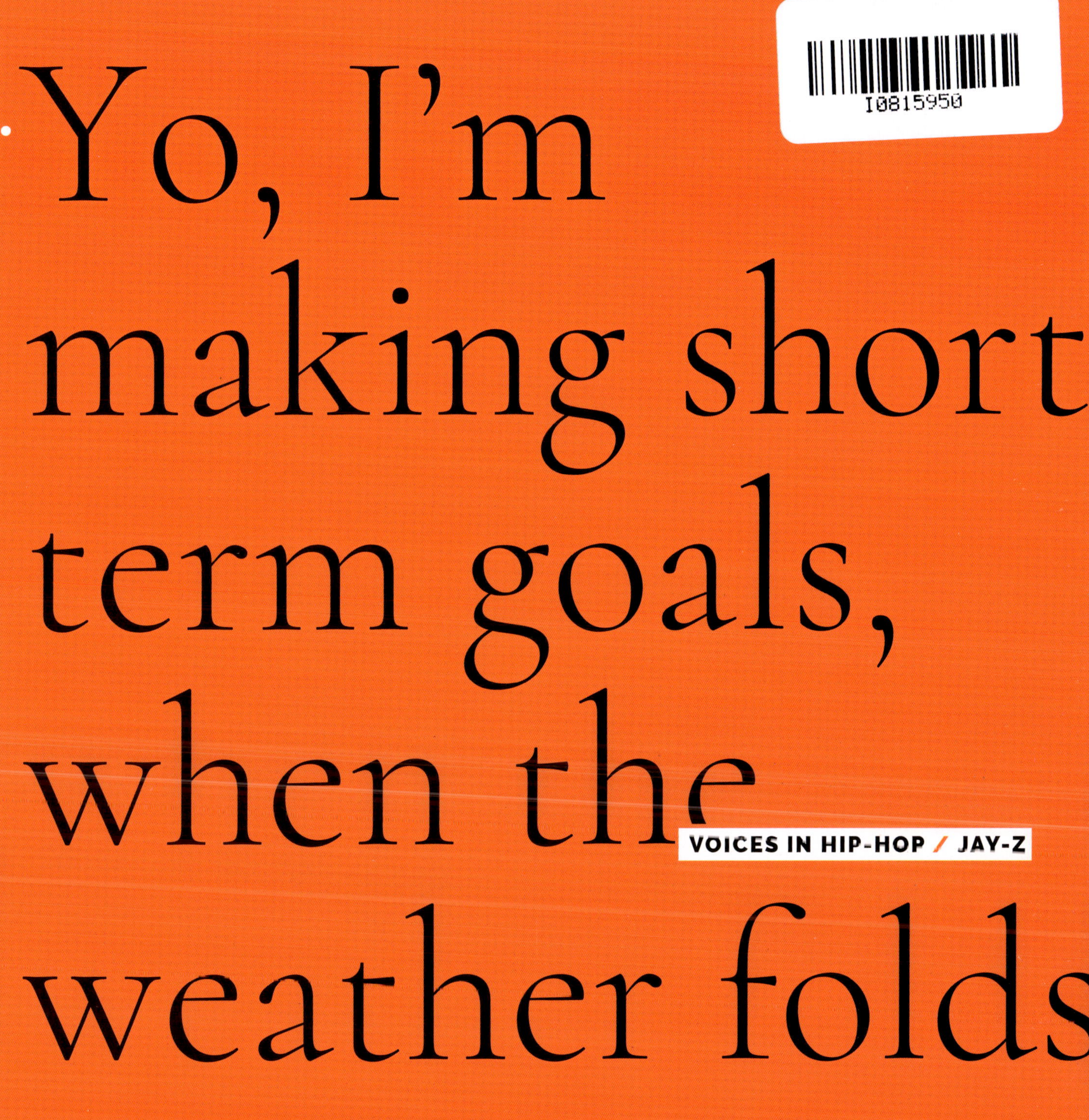
Yo, I'm
making short
term goals,
when the
VOICES IN HIP-HOP / JAY-Z
weather folds

Just put

VOICES IN HIP-HOP

JAY-Z

CATE RUBENSTEIN

CREATIVE EDUCATION / CREATIVE PAPERBACKS

Jay-Z and Bi

n— s— your

(Wher

Brookl

(Marcy)Tha

don't stop

Published by Creative Education and Creative Paperbacks
P.O. Box 227, Mankato, Minnesota 56002
Creative Education and Creative Paperbacks are
imprints of The Creative Company
www.thecreativecompany.us

Design by Tom Morgan
Art direction by Blue Design (www.bluedes.com)

Images by Dreamstime/Chris Giroux, 9, Fabio Diena, 16, Kraft74, 28, Michael Bush, cover, 3, 10, 21; Getty Images/Kevin Mazur/MTV1415, 36, Nitro, 12, Rune Hellestad - Corbis, 2, Timothy Nwachukwu, 40; Wikimedia Commons/i am guilty, 23, Joella Marano, 32, Mikamote, 18–19, wonker, 22
Every effort has been made to contact copyright holders for material reproduced in this book. Any omissions will be rectified in subsequent printings if notice is given to the publisher.

Library of Congress Cataloging-in-Publication Data
Names: Rubenstein, Cate, author.
Title: Jay-Z / by Cate Rubenstein.
Description: Mankato, Minnesota : Creative Education and Creative Paperbacks, 2026. | Series: Voices in hip-hop | Includes index. | Audience: Ages 12–15 | Audience: Grades 7–9 | Summary: "Listen up! It's Jay-Z, the business savvy hip-hop artist. Part biography, part song lyric collection, this music-fueled title for high school readers celebrates the rapper's journey and voice. Includes a selected discography and index"– Provided by publisher.
Identifiers: LCCN 2024055855 (print) | LCCN 2024055856 (ebook) | ISBN 9798889892793 (library binding) | ISBN 9781682776452 (paperback) | ISBN 9798889893905 (ebook)
Subjects: LCSH: Jay-Z, 1969– –Juvenile literature. | Rap musicians–United States–Biography–Juvenile literature.
Classification: LCC ML3930.J38 R83 2026 (print) | LCC ML3930.J38 (ebook) | DDC 782.421649092 [B]–dc23/eng/20241120
LC record available at https://lccn.loc.gov/2024055855
LC ebook record available at https://lccn.loc.gov/2024055856

Printed in India

gie Smalls,
drawers
rom?)
n' out for all
's right, you

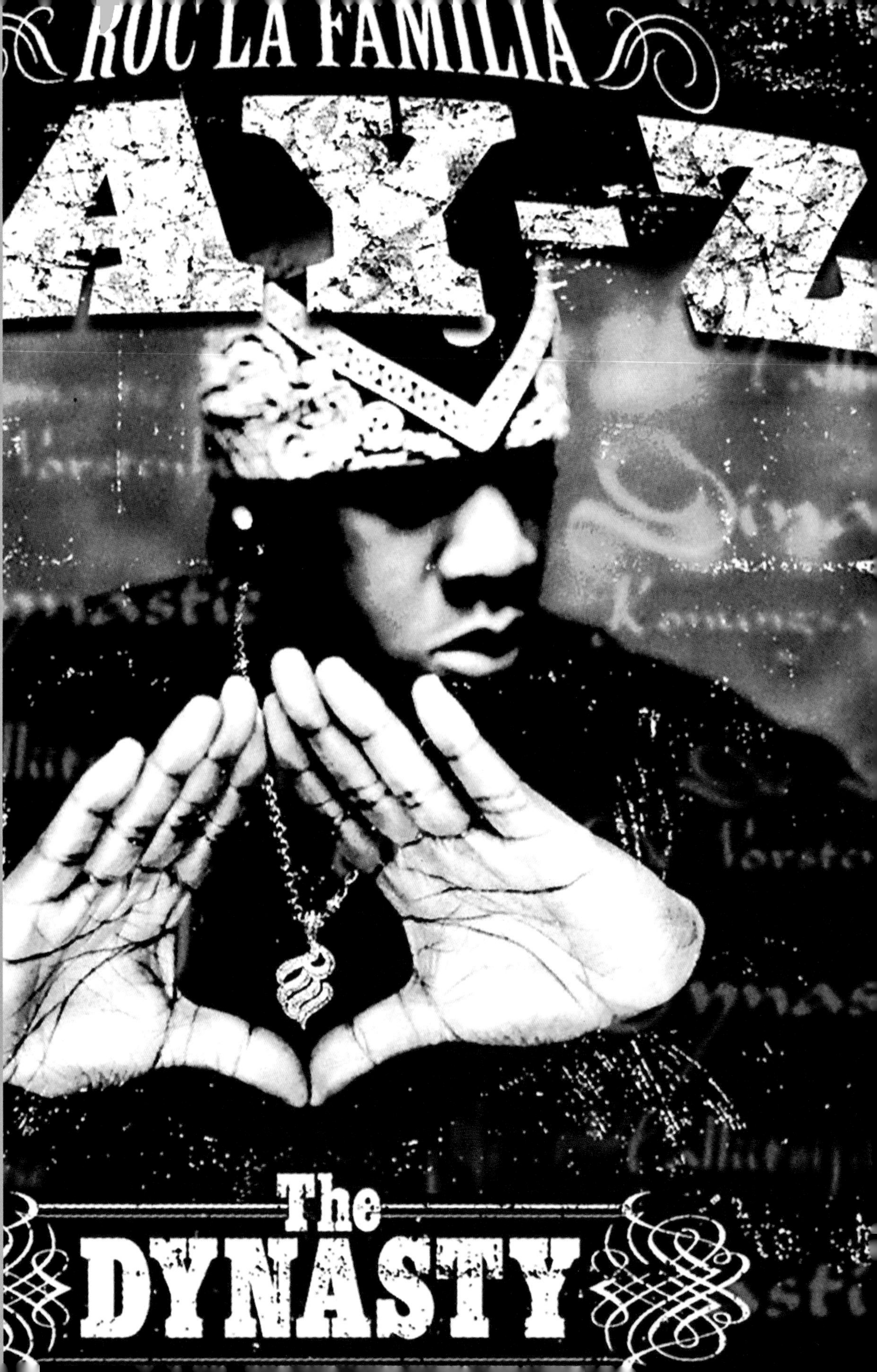
ROC LA FAMILIA
The
DYNASTY

contents

• • •

Foreword

• • •

Jay-Z and Biggie Smalls, n— s— your drawers
(Where you from?) Brooklyn, goin' out for all
(Marcy) That's right, you don't stop
(Bed-Stuy) You won't stop (n—)
What, what, what?

—FROM "BROOKLYN'S FINEST" ON THE 1996 ALBUM *REASONABLE DOUBT*

"Not only is he an entirely self-made man, he's found his great success doing exactly what he loves. He is thoughtful and intelligent, a reader and a seeker."

—OPRAH WINFREY ABOUT JAY-Z, *O, THE OPRAH MAGAZINE*, 2009

Introduction

• • •

Jay-Z makes no secret of his past in the mean streets. In fact, it's been a key element in his storytelling, from growing up in the Marcy Projects to headlining sold-out shows at Madison Square Garden. His childhood was brutally devoid of innocence and almost mythologically riddled with difficulties. Yet somehow he still managed to escape his beginnings to become the superstar he is today. With nothing on his side but hustle, he went on to become one of the best rappers of all time and a billionaire businessman, with catchy music known worldwide for his confessional, tell-all style of rapping.

Called "relentlessly autobiographical," Jay-Z tells his story like it was—the neglected teen selling drugs, failed relationships, failed friendships, rivalries, the grind of his lifestyle, nonstop striving to go farther and get more, unchecked appetite for material objects—and epic, unparalleled, meteoric success. All 13 of his studio albums were certified platinum. He was the first Black male artist to go multi-platinum more than 10 times. He is the second most-nominated artist in Grammy history. He is an entrepreneur many times over across multiple realms of business. He is married to, and parenting with, another global supernova: Beyoncé. On its face, he has everything and more than he could ever have wished for as a child in Marcy. What drives him still, though, is connecting his music to kids who remind him of himself: kids who weren't born with the proverbial silver spoon, kids with all odds stacked against them. He never forgot where he came from, and hopes to inspire through being honest about how bad things were for him once. He hopes kids can see that if he made it out of his situation, they can, too. Frequently brash and eminently bleep-able, his lyrics don't shy away from swagger and posturing. Yet, underneath the bravado, at times he's almost tender, rapping with great sensitivity, nuance, self-awareness, and understanding of how he comes across to people, and how the world sees him.

The Notorious B.I.G. and Jay-Z, circa 1996

Early Years

•••

"Some people are attracted to vulnerability. From my very first album, I've been vulnerable. I've always given parts of me, parts of my life—good, bad, ugly."

—JAY-Z, ***BRITISH GQ***, 2005

Shawn Corey Carter was born on December 4, 1969, in Brooklyn, New York, to Adnis Reeves and Gloria Carter. Raised in the Bedford-Stuyvesant ("Bed-Stuy") neighborhood, he moved into Marcy at age five with his parents and three siblings: Eric, Annie, and Mickey.

On stage with rapper Nas in 2019, Jay-Z likened growing up in the projects to crabs in a barrel: "You've seen crabs trying to get out of the barrel? They pull each other down, trying to get up. They're just grabbing at whatever they can. People are at the point where they're ready to do anything, so it's very dangerous. And you're living in close quarters, so you have to deal with danger every day, from every angle."

MARCY PROJECTS

The Marcy Projects opened in 1949, as part of an effort to house New York City's low-income residents. The affordable housing complex, named after U.S. statesman William Marcy, is located on the original site of a Dutch windmill in Brooklyn. By the 1970s, the 27 six-story buildings in the complex had fallen into dangerous disrepair. The projects became infamous for drug violence, drug use, and domestic violence. In recent years, the complex has been part of urban renewal efforts.

Reportedly witnessing a murder at age nine, he was also nine when he "started messing" with his parents' record player. Rapt with joy seeing hip-hop group The Sugarhill Gang on *Soul Train*—the first American music TV show to prominently feature Black musical acts and dancers—Shawn was inspired to make beats of his own.

Around that same time, his father started using heroin. Not much later, he abandoned the family when Shawn was 11. Lacking a father figure, drug dealers became Shawn's role models. They offered a high-rolling lifestyle and imbued in him a code of "ethics."

"On the streets, you had to operate with integrity," he told Oprah Winfrey in 2009. "If you broke your word to someone, he wasn't going to take you to court—he was going to deal with you himself. So it was here in the projects that I learned loyalty."

Life was a struggle, daily. "It was a very intense and stressful situation," Jay-Z said on the National Public Radio (NPR) show *Fresh Air* in 2010. "There was playing in the Johnny-pump and the ice-cream man coming around and all of these games that we'd play, and suddenly it would turn just violent and there would be shootings at 12 in the afternoon on any given day. It was a weird mix of emotions. One day, your best friend could be killed. The day before, you could be celebrating him getting a brand-new bike."

riven by poverty, Shawn started selling crack at 13. He carried a gun, and he found himself in a number of tense situations. On one occasion, he shot his older brother in front of their sisters, deliberately and at close range. On another occasion, he got shot by a friend over a "misunderstanding." Dealing drugs for almost a decade, he avows: "No one aspires to be a drug dealer . . . You aspire to the lifestyle you see around you. You see the green BMW, the prettiest car you've ever seen. You see the trappings of drug dealing, and it draws you in. At 14–15 years old, you're thinking about sneakers, or you're thinking about some sort of relief from all of the pain you're feeling. You're thinking about buying some food for the house. You're thinking about paying the extra light bill. So at that young age, you're not thinking about the destruction you're causing your own community."

Yo, I'm making short term goals, when the weather folds
Just put away the leathers and put ice on the gold
Chilly with enough bail money to free a big Willy
High stakes, I got more at stake than Philly

—FROM "CAN'T KNOCK THE HUSTLE" ON THE 1996 ALBUM *REASONABLE DOUBT*

School

• • •

"I'm a thinker. I figure things out. I don't have a high level of education, but I'm practical—and I have good instincts."

—JAY-Z, *O, THE OPRAH MAGAZINE*, 2009

Shawn was an excellent student. His favorite class was English. He found escape in language. Teachers remember him as a reader and daydreamer, a quiet, withdrawn kid with his nose in a book. In 6th grade he tested at a 12th grade reading level. His favorite teacher told him: "You're smart, you better do well." Later, Shawn called her "someone who helped turn my life around. She took our class to her house in Brooklyn on a field trip, you know many teachers who'd take a bunch of Black kids to their house?" Seeing ice in her freezer, Shawn thought being an English teacher must pay well and considered it his potential future. His favorite books ranged from the dictionary to Homer's *The Odyssey* and Gary Zukav's *The Seat of the Soul*. His love for words and sentence structure began to drive him lyrically.

Stability was scarce, but music was a steady backbeat. His parents' record collection exposed him early to Michael Jackson, Stevie Wonder, and Motown, with *Soul Train* continually on TV. Winning a freestyle rap contest against fellow up-and-coming rapper Busta Rhymes in their high school cafeteria was a highlight. Losing a rap contest judged by rapper LL Cool J was disappointing. After attempting three different high schools and despite how promising his academics looked, Shawn dropped out of high school during his sophomore year and was soon full-time dealing.

When he wasn't out on the streets hustling, his newfound friendship with rapper and record producer Jaz-O was quickly becoming a flourishing musical apprenticeship. Jaz-O even took young Shawn to London to make an album. The album was technically a success. The record label instantly wanted to sign Shawn. But he refused, saying music executives had no integrity, and he'd rather keep dealing. So he went back to selling drugs on the streets. All the while, though, he was still rhyming. He wrote new material down in a green notebook he always carried around with him.

CLASSICS

...Throughout my life (uh hu
uh huh uh)

..No matter what I've don
(right)

Growing Up

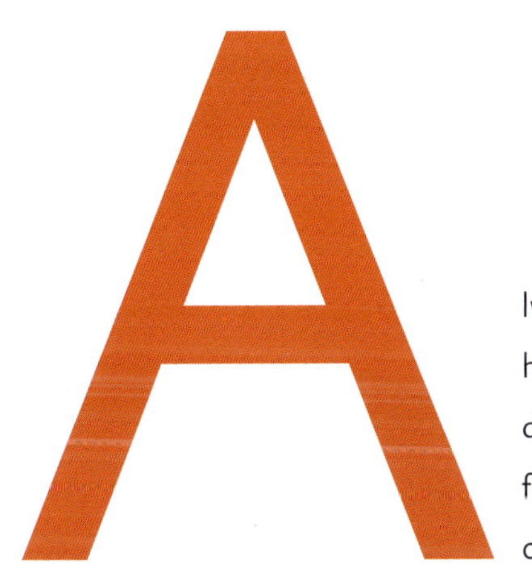lways close to his mother, Gloria, Shawn credits her with all of his strength. His father's departure deeply scarred him. He felt abandoned and furious. In later years, he would come to a place of empathy for what his father had been going through. He would recognize his father's actions as an inability to cope, rather than a personally directed lack of love. Forgiveness from his older brother, after being shot by the then-12-year-old Shawn, also affected him greatly. He rapped about it in "You Must Love Me."

Throughout my life (uh huh uh huh uh)
No matter what I've done (right)
You've been merciful and your love endureth (yeah)

Through all things (yeah)
For that I am eternally grateful

—FROM "YOU MUST LOVE ME" ON THE 1997 ALBUM *IN MY LIFETIME, VOL 1.*

The crack epidemic of the 1980s and early 1990s affected how Shawn saw authority. "It changed the authority figure," he told NPR. "Crack cocaine was done so openly, and the people who were addicted to it, the fiends, had very little self-respect. It was so highly addictive that they didn't care how they obtained it, and they carried that out in front of children, who were dealing. So, 'I have to respect my elders' . . . that dynamic shifted, and it broke forever. It just changed everything from that point on."

He recognized he lacked awareness for a long while of the harm he was causing by dealing drugs. "So deep in it, and so young, that type of introspection never happens," he told Oprah. "It's just living. And it's fast."

As time passed, everyone he knew was ending up in jail and/or dead, so he began to realize there wasn't a happy ending to the lifestyle he was leading and glamorizing.

From Streets to Stardom

• • •

Around age 20, Shawn started trying to transition from the streets to music, but it proved harder than he thought to quit the drug-dealing lifestyle. He'd make incredible demos, then get sidetracked for months in the grind of dealing and hustling. Eventually, he realized he couldn't be successful unless he let go of the street life completely.

Instead of selling drugs, he then started selling his own records out of his car. He launched Roc-A-Fella Records in 1994. Two years later, his debut album *Reasonable Doubt* hit stores nationwide, and the name Jay-Z was launched. The

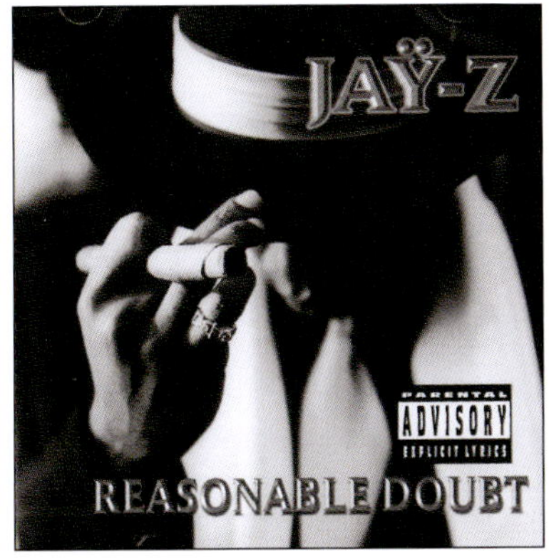

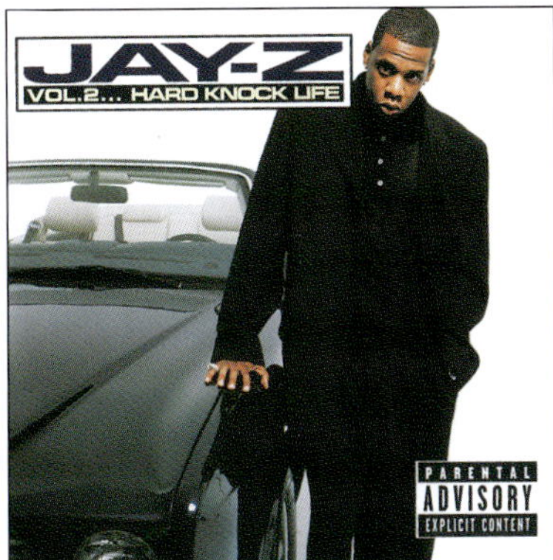

name was a play on a childhood nickname, "Jazzy," a homage to his friend Jaz-O, and, last but not least, a shoutout to the J/Z subway station near Marcy. His personal favorite album, *Reasonable Doubt* charted on the Billboard 200, certified multi-platinum, and was named one of *Rolling Stone's* "500 Greatest Albums of All Time."

At the height of this fresh success, former schoolmate Biggie Smalls (also known as The Notorious B.I.G.) was gunned down. Biggie was an enormous influence on Shawn musically, and a close friend. In fact, they'd even chatted on the phone the night Biggie was shot. His death was devastating and impacted Shawn greatly. It inspired him to keep making music and work through feelings.

In 1998, Jay-Z released his explosive hit "Hard Knock Life (Ghetto Anthem)." It was inspired by the musical *Annie*. "I was drawn to it [*Annie*]," Jay-Z told NPR. "It was the struggle of this poor kid in this environment and how her life changed. It immediately resonated."

Determined to secure rights for the beloved musical lyrics to "Hard Knock Life," Jay-Z wrote *Annie* songwriters Charles Strouse and Martin Charnin. He used his way with words to tell them how much *Annie* had meant to him as a child, even claiming he had won an essay contest and gone to see the musical on Broadway, which he said cemented his enduring love for the story. He would later admit he made it all up—he actually saw *Annie* on TV.

VOICES IN
HIP-HOP

How People Saw Him

espite his tremendous success, some lamented Jay-Z's lyrics for glamorizing violence. "There's something real there," he admitted to *British GQ* in 2005. But he went on to say: "How are all these guns in these neighborhoods? How are all these drugs in these neighborhoods? It makes me sad that all this only becomes a problem when it reaches the suburbs."

Critics also noted that many of Jay-Z's lyrics belittled women, the Jewish community, and the Black community, with flagrant misogyny, antisemitism, and use of the "n-word."

Z THE BLACK ALBU

On misogyny, he blames rap generally, saying: "A lot of these albums are made when artists are young, 17 or 18 years old, so they've never had any real relationships. And if you come from the neighborhoods we're in, we have low esteem ourselves. And the women, well, the girls—they have low self-esteem, as well. These are all dysfunctional relationships at a young age. The poet is pretty much [giving] his take on his dealings with girls at that time. He's not in a stable relationship; he's on the road. He's seeing girls who like him because he makes music. They spend one night together; he gets a phone number. He leaves for the next town and does the same thing over again."

As for antisemitism, he defends his lyrics about one of the oldest conspiracy theories of Jewish people—that they control the world's money—which they don't—by underscoring he's harsh on his own community, too.

On the n-word, he agrees it isn't necessary, but also insists: "It's just become part of the way we communicate. My generation hasn't had the same experience with that word that generations of people before us had. We weren't so close to the pain. So in our way, we disarmed the word. We took the fire pin out of the grenade."

Success Level Unlocked

• • •

Rap and hip-hop have gone through many different iterations. While the 1990s were considered by many to be the golden era, with innovation, creativity and cultural impact at an all-time high, the music continues to this day to influence industries from fashion to politics, from technology to art to language. Early artists in the genre showcased urban devastation, with neighborhoods ruined by drugs and crime. By the time Jay-Z came around, it was "all Bentleys and babes and pool parties in Miami. What happened?" Rising out of poverty and the streets was not easy, and Jay-Z's lyrics revel in all the trappings of success that come with fame and excess. He explains: "It's more of a celebration than showing off. It's more like, 'Yo, I got money! Oh, s—! Throw it in the air! Pour some Cristal out!' You have to realize that most of us come from nothing, like no-thing, the bottom. You start getting some success, you're gonna start celebrating it. And because you're on TV, the whole world sees you celebrating."

While recognizing that a lot of rap historically was meant to be aspirational, with artists rapping about the big house they wanted one day, the fame, the cars, and the accolades, he notes with continued self-awareness the personal difference in being well beyond survival. No longer was he in it to feed his family, but because he radically enjoyed his riches, and buying cars and jewelry. Improbably, he had managed to re-invent himself.

Life Happens

R*easonable Doubt* was an unparalleled and enormous success. But it didn't stop there. The albums kept coming.

The Blueprint was released in 2001, covering numerous breakups and his inability to access his emotions fully. His father's abandonment had made him seal off emotionally. "When you're growing up, your dad is your superhero," he told Oprah. "Once you've let yourself fall that in love with someone, once you put him on such a high pedestal and he lets you down, you never want to experience that pain again. So I remember just being really quiet and really cold. Never wanting to let myself get close to someone like that again. I carried that feeling throughout my life."

Considered one of the greatest hip-hop albums of all time, *The Blueprint* was certified three times multi-platinum by the Recording Industry Association of

Jay-Z and his mom, Gloria Carter

America (RIAA). For its cultural significance, it was the first entry of the 21st century to be included in the Library of Congress National Recording Industry Registry.

But 2001 was not an easy time for Jay-Z generally. He was arrested and charged with criminal possession of a weapon in the third degree. He also pleaded guilty to stabbing a record executive at a Manhattan nightclub, and he was subsequently sentenced to three years' probation. He feuded publicly with rival rapper Nas.

In 2002, things started looking up when Jay-Z collaborated with Beyoncé on "'03 Bonnie & Clyde." He also appeared in the hit single "Crazy in Love" on her debut album *Dangerously in Love* (2003). The song topped the Billboard Hot 100 chart.

In 2003, Jay-Z reconciled with his estranged father, just months before Adnis died of liver failure on the same night Jay-Z opened the 40/40 Club (Jay-Z's sports bar chain). Finally, Jay-Z got to tell Adnis how hurt he was all those years before when Adnis left the family, and that it was Adnis's responsibility to have tried hard to stay in his son's life. "Reconnecting with my father changed me more than anything, because it allowed me to let people in," Jay-Z told Oprah. "When I was a kid, I once waited for him on a bench. He never showed up. Even as an adult, that affected me. So when my mom set up this meeting, I told her he wouldn't come—and the first time, he didn't. At that point, I was really done, but Mom pushed for another meeting, because she's just a beautiful soul."

Jay-Z then retired (temporarily) that year, with a giant farewell show at Madison Square Garden in New York City featuring many fellow popular artists—the Roots, Missy Elliott, Mary J. Blige, Beyoncé, and Pharrell Williams. In a lavish display of generosity, all proceeds were donated to charity.

Back to Business

Retirement didn't last long, though. In 2004, Jay-Z was back—this time as president and chief executive officer of Def Jam. Soon, other signed talent became household names. Rihanna, Shakira, Kanye West, and Kyrie Irving were some of the best known new recruits. *The Black Album,* which Jay-Z released in 2004, debuted as number one on the Billboard 200. Certified quadruple platinum by RIAA, it became his top-selling album of the decade. Jay-Z also became part owner of the Brooklyn Nets basketball team.

In 2006, former Beatle Sir Paul McCartney unofficially "knighted" Jay-Z with his sword as "Sir Hova of Brooklyn." Technically, only British monarchs can knight British citizens. However, McCartney himself was knighted previously, hence affectionately decided to express his appreciation for Jay-Z's genius in this same way. "Hova" is a play on "Jay-Hova," another nickname for Jay-Z.

In 2007, Jay-Z collaborated with Pantone and GMC Yukon Denali, on his own shade of blue for the luxury car. "Jay-Z Blue" is a pearly blue mixed with platinum dust. His album *American Gangster,* released the same year, debuted as number one on the Billboard 200 and was certified platinum by RIAA a month after its release.

More success followed in 2008, when he founded Roc Nation. The organization spanned music, sports, talent management, publishing, and distribution. It aimed to promote and support diverse artists and athletes, ensuring they had creative and financial control over their careers.

Barack Obama's 2008 election as president was another seminal moment. "The day that Barack Obama became president, the gangsta became less relevant," Jay-Z told Oprah. "We grew up without accountants and lawyers as role models, but now we see something different. There's something else for us to aspire to."

It was a big year for Jay-Z personally, as well. After keeping their six-year relationship quiet, he and Beyoncé married in a private ceremony in Tribeca, an upscale neighborhood in New York City.

In 2009, Jay-Z released his 11th studio album *The Blueprint 3.* With it, he broke Elvis' record for most number-one albums ever by a solo artist. The single "Empire State of Mind" (featuring Alicia Keys) topped the Billboard Hot 100 for five consecutive weeks, becoming Jay-Z's first number-one single as a lead artist.

His book *Memoir Decoded* was released in 2010. Ironically for the rapper known for his tell-all style, the book was seen as not personal enough.

Coasting on success, in 2015, Jay-Z bought music streaming service Tidal. He signed a 10-year, $200-million touring partnership with Live Nation, an entertainment company resulting from the merger of Live Nation and Ticketmaster. He was named *GQ*'s International Man of the Year.

In 2017, his mother came out as a lesbian, which Jay-Z supported fully with his song "Smile" on the album *4:44*: "Mama had four kids, but she's a lesbian/Had to pretend so long that she's a thespian." LGBTQ advocacy organization GLAAD would honor Jay-Z and Beyoncé in 2019 for their joint role in accelerating LGBTQ acceptance, quite a rare thing in hip-hop.

JAY-Z AND BEYONCÉ

Friends for a couple of years before dating, Jay-Z and Beyoncé met when she was just 18. While keeping a very low profile as a couple initially, they strode the red carpet together in 2004 at the MTV Video Music Awards in Miami, Florida. The couple has declined to speak openly about each other, though they very publicly work through marital issues in their music and are frequently spotted together. They welcomed daughter Blue Ivy (pictured with parents) in 2012 and twins Sir and Rumi in 2017.

Behind the Scenes

Do I find it so hard
When I know in my heart
I'm letting you down every day
Letting you down every day

—FROM "4:44" ON THE 2017 ALBUM *4:44*

Jay-Z worked through personal dramas in his music. "I don't want to say it's therapy because everyone says that, but it is," he told *British GQ*. "I'm not a person who has tremendous highs or lows. I don't get depressed, and you'll never catch me jumping around, extra happy. And that can be dangerous to you. Sometimes I'll hold stuff in. But doing raps, I get to talk through it, I get to deal with a lot of things."

His confessional style made listeners feel they really knew him, and it was also a way for him to better know himself. His songs explored the deep hurts he was carrying: abandonment, poverty fueling his decisions, the stillborn baby an ex-girlfriend birthed, his infamous infidelity that sent Beyoncé to the brink . . . During Beyoncé's pregnancy with their first child, he rapped in "New Day" on his 2011 album *Watch the Throne* with Kanye West: "My dad left me and I promise never repeat him." Jay-Z had to re-examine all his behavior with women in light of how his daughter might see it someday when she was grown up enough to know and understand what happened. He admits he didn't have the emotional tools for marriage, but was working on himself to get them. He told *The New York Times* in 2017: "The hardest thing is seeing pain on someone's face that you caused, and then have to deal with yourself."

"When you make music, you're constantly on the psychiatrist's couch, so to speak. That's an outlet for me. Because I'm not normally a talkative person."

—JAY-Z, *O, THE OPRAH MAGAZINE*, 2009

Recent Work

His latest album, *4:44*, lost a lot of his earlier façade and swagger. The lyrics are contemplative, thoughtful, and find him more open, honest, filled with regrets, and troubled by understanding he caused multiple women real pain and doesn't know how to do better. It's widely considered a supremely strong effort that easily eclipses much of his earlier work.

"The Story of O.J." contains powerful lyrics expressing his conflicted thoughts about success, and his frustration that, regardless of his fame and riches, he won't transcend racism.

Skin is, skin is
Skin black, my skin is black
My, black, my skin is yellow
Light n—, dark n—, faux n—, real n—
Rich n—, poor n—, house n—, field n—
Still n—, still n—

—FROM "THE STORY OF O.J." ON THE 2017 ALBUM *4:44*

Giving Back

• • •

aving achieved all the material goods anyone could ever want, Jay-Z turned his attention to the community at large. Roc Nation signed a partnership deal with the National Football League (NFL) to provide entertainment for Super Bowl halftime shows. This helped the NFL's "Inspire Change" social justice initiative to lower barriers to opportunity for people of color. In 2018, Jay-Z also went on *The Late Show with David Letterman* to advocate for better teacher wages. He established the Shawn Carter Scholarship Fund for disadvantaged and formerly incarcerated youth who hope to attend college, and he worked with the United Nations to raise awareness of global water shortages.

Skin is, skin i
Skin black, m
skin is black
My, black, my
skin is yellow
Light n—, dar

Continued Success

In 2019, Jay-Z was the world's first rapper to become a billionaire. Revenues streamed in from Rocawear, a hip-hop streetwear brand; liquor brand deals; his stake in the Nets; another stake in ride-share service Uber; partnership with the NFL; endorsement deals with sneaker brand Reebok and luxury watchmaker Audemars-Piguet; and multiple other businesses. As he had said himself in "Diamonds From Sierra Leone" on the 2005 Kanye West album *Late Registration*, "I'm not a businessman. I'm a business, man."

Add "real-estate mogul" to the list. No strangers to rarefied purchases, in 2023, he and Beyoncé bought the most expensive home ever sold in California, a $200-million-dollar Malibu estate. He also picked up an Emmy win for directing

Rihanna in the Super Bowl LVII (57) halftime show, then won the Dr. Dre Global Impact Award at the 2024 Grammys.

Somewhere along the way, he became quite a collector, not just of real estate but of art. There's an original painting by American neo-expressionist artist Basquiat in his kitchen, and that's only one part of his costly art collection. Additionally, he owns more than one island and enjoys sprawling properties in both New York and Los Angeles.

Retirement, Redux?

It's been years since Jay-Z's last album, but don't count him out. He's said rap is a young man's sport, but his career and business moves indicate that he is here for the long haul. As he told *The New York Times,* "You know what I mean; like, you rather be a trend, or you rather be forever?"

At his level, Jay-Z doesn't need to make an album every year just to stay relevant. He's an icon. "It got to a point where I was making an album every year, making an album just to make an album," he told *British GQ.* "I never wanted to do it for that. I wanted to always be passionate about it. And the music around me wasn't inspiring. Like when Big [Biggie Smalls, The Notorious B.I.G.] was around, I'd listen to one of his songs and I'd be like, 'That's f—ing great,' and I would make ten records trying to best his record."

It's highly possible his next effort will do what he's always done: reflect where he is at that moment in life, and what's happening. "I'm a mirror," he's said. "Smile into the mirror, you'll get smiles back. Throw insults into the mirror, you'll get insults back."

Success has found him philosophical about what that word really means. "It's not about who got more money and who got more houses," he told NPR. "Yes, you know, you've earned it, buy what you want . . . But don't forget what's important. Without people, being rich would be very boring."

"Rap is what took me out of my situation, and now I must care for it. I have to leave it as I found it—or better—for the next generation of kids. Then maybe they can change their situation like I did."

—JAY-Z INTERVIEW WITH OPRAH WINFREY, *O, THE OPRAH MAGAZINE*, 2009

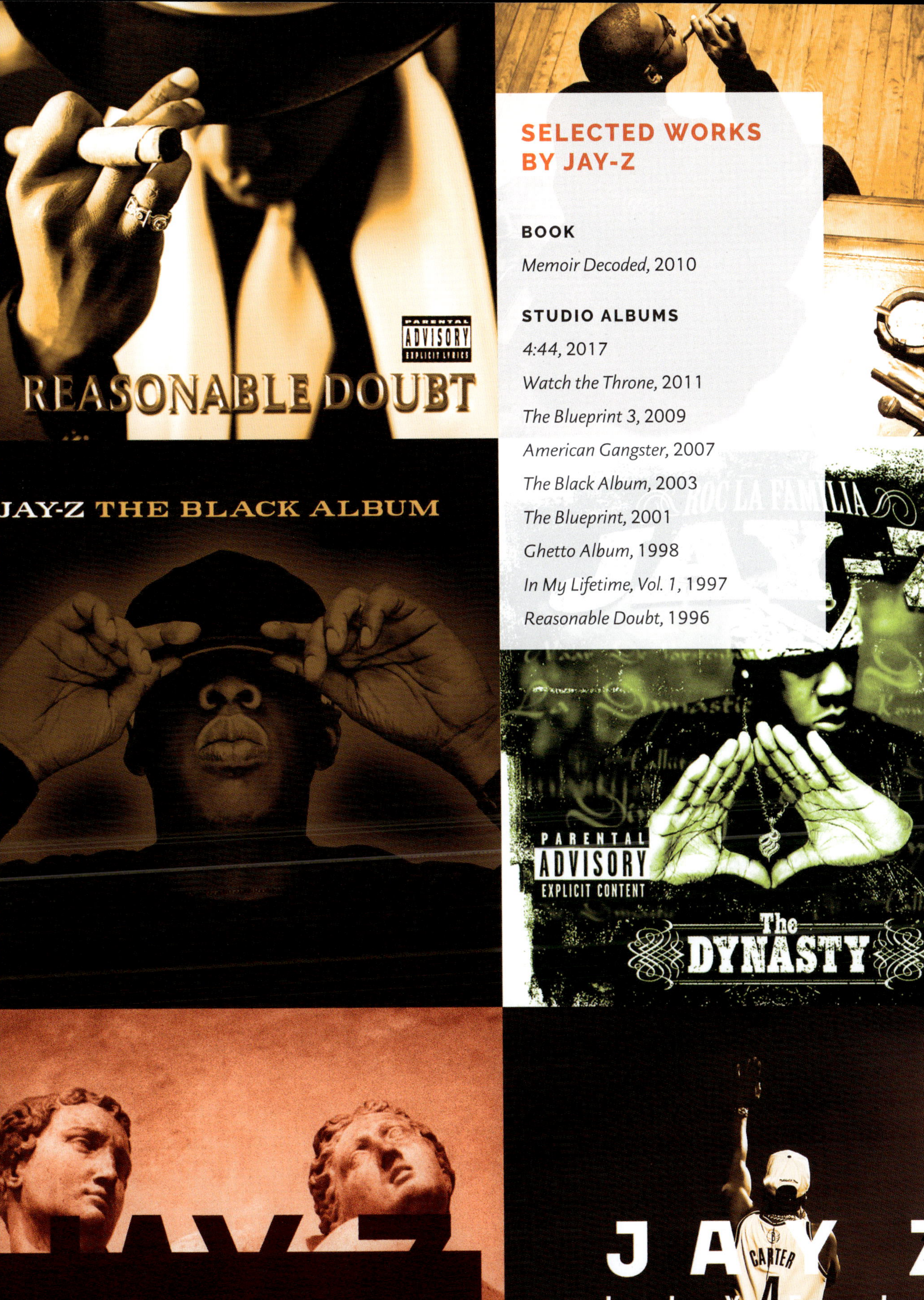

SELECTED WORKS BY JAY-Z

BOOK

Memoir Decoded, 2010

STUDIO ALBUMS

4:44, 2017

Watch the Throne, 2011

The Blueprint 3, 2009

American Gangster, 2007

The Black Album, 2003

The Blueprint, 2001

Ghetto Album, 1998

In My Lifetime, Vol. 1, 1997

Reasonable Doubt, 1996

INDEX